HAND PRINTS

ARTY Crafty

CAROLYN
SCRACE

WITH SIMPLE STEP-BY-STEP INSTRUCTIONS

BOOK HOUSE
a SALARIYA imprint

This edition first published in MMXX by
Book House

Distributed by Black Rabbit Books
P.O. Box 3263
Mankato, Minnesota 56002

Cataloging-in-Publication Data is available
from the Library of Congress

Printed in the United States
At Corporate Graphics,
North Mankato, Minnesota

9 8 7 6 5 4 3 2 1

ISBN: 978-1-912904-29-7

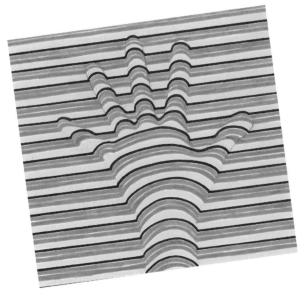

CONTENTS

WHAT YOU NEED

The crafts in this book use materials that you can find in art shops, craft stores, and around your home. This page shows you the materials you will need to make the ideas in this book.

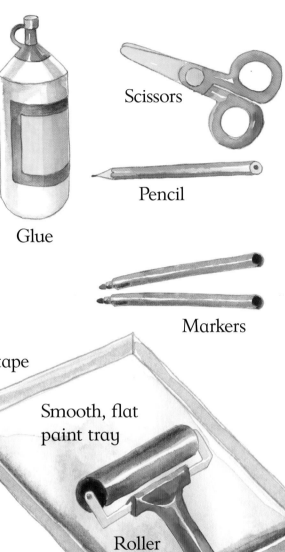

Glue

Scissors

Pencil

Markers

Colored paper

Sticky tape

Smooth, flat paint tray

Ruler

Ribbon

Roller

Paints

Plate

Paintbrush

Follow the simple step-by-step guides to create lots of wonderful results! Find out how to make a scary Dracula handprint, a footprint snowman, and much, much more.

LET'S GET STARTED!

5

HOW TO PRINT
Fingers, Thumbs, Hands, and Feet

SIMPLE THUMBPRINTS

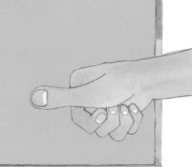

1 Put some paint onto a plate, and have a clean sheet of paper ready. Place your thumb (or finger) in the paint to coat it.

2 Press your thumb firmly down on the paper and lift it off.

3 Make some more prints then leave to dry. Wash your hand and the plate.

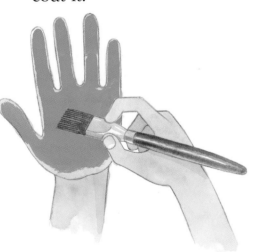

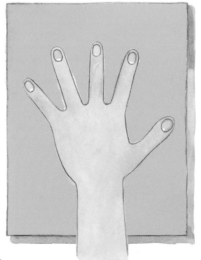

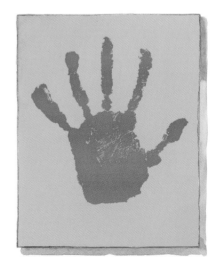

4 Paint the palm of your hand (or sole of your foot) using a paintbrush.

2 Quickly place your hand (or foot) onto a clean sheet of paper. Press down firmly.

3 Peel off the paper and leave the print to dry. Wash your hands and the brush and plate.

6

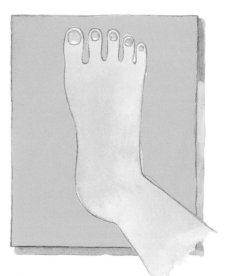

1 Add some paint to a tray then run the roller back and forth until it is evenly covered.

2 Roll it over the sole of your foot (or the palm of your hand).

3 Step (or put the palm of your hand) onto a clean sheet of paper.

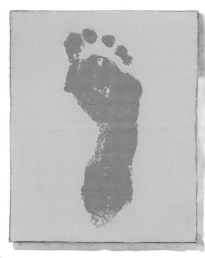

4 Peel off the paper and leave the print to dry. Wash off all the remaining paint.

Study your finished prints for inspiration. You could design a scary monster, a red rooster, or a little bird?

7

VEHICLE Footprints

Putt... Putt...

TRACTOR

1 Make a blue footprint. Leave to dry.

2 Now cut wheels out of paper. To make tractor wheels, cut out small sections (as shown).

3 Cut out two inner disks. Glue the tractor wheels onto your artwork, then add the inner disks.

4 Cut the roof shape from paper, and three thin strips to make the windows. Glue in place.

5 Use a black marker to draw in the steering wheel, wheel nuts, and headlights.

SOME MORE FOOTPRINT VEHICLES FOR YOU TO TRY!

Eeee Aww

FIRE ENGINE

Vroom Vroom

CAR

SNOWMAN
Footprint

To make this decoration, cut out the shape of the snowman. Make a hole in the top and thread some ribbon through.

1. Take a sheet of blue paper and use white paint to make a footprint. Leave to dry.

2. Cut the shapes of the snowman's hat and scarf out of colored paper.

3. Glue the hat and scarf in place. Cut and glue colored paper strips to the scarf.

4. Cut out a pink carrot-shaped nose and his stick-like arms. Glue in place.

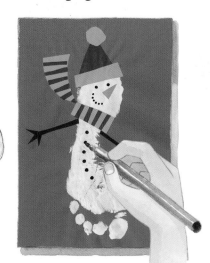

5. Use a marker to draw in his eyes and mouth, and a row of buttons for his coat.

A PAIR OF SNOWMEN

11

FESTIVE WREATH
Handprints

1 Use a dinner plate to draw a circle on a piece of thick paper.

2 Now make a smaller circle using a side plate (as shown).

3 Cut around both rings to make a doughnut shape.

4 This paper ring is the base of the wreath.

5 Now make lots of green and red handprints.

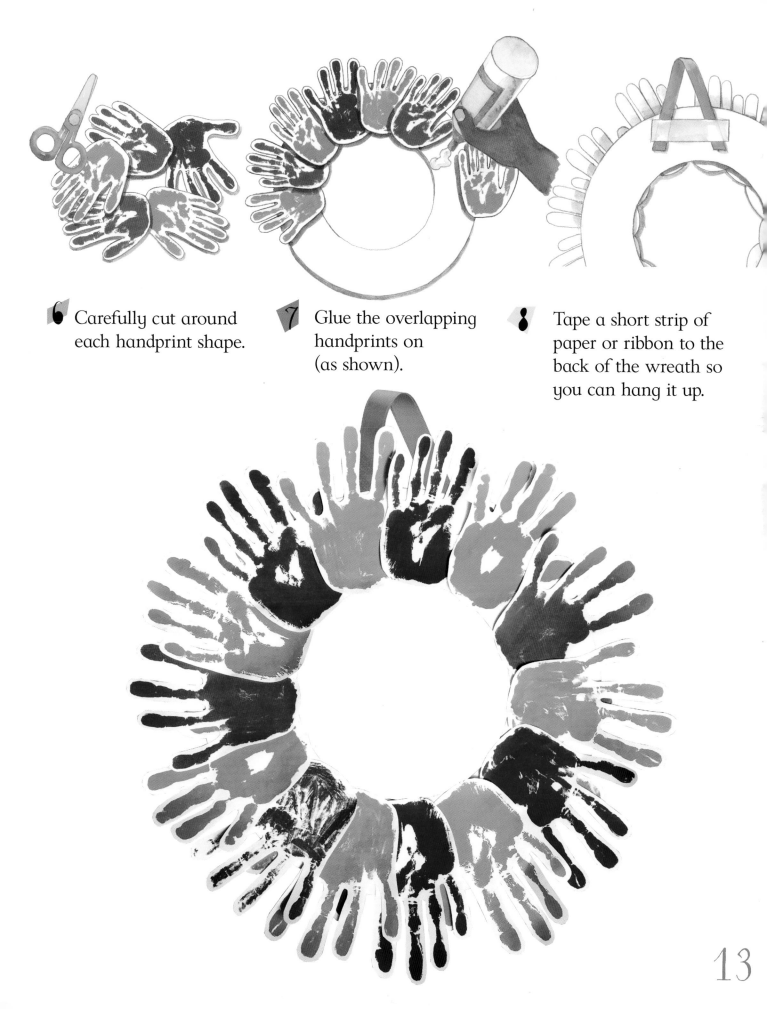

6 Carefully cut around each handprint shape.

7 Glue the overlapping handprints on (as shown).

8 Tape a short strip of paper or ribbon to the back of the wreath so you can hang it up.

TREE
Handprint

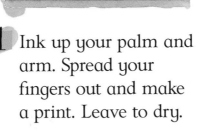

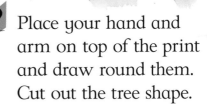

1 Ink up your palm and arm. Spread your fingers out and make a print. Leave to dry.

2 Place your hand and arm on top of the print and draw round them. Cut out the tree shape.

3 Glue the tree shape in place onto a large sheet of paper.

4 Mix up some green paints and start adding fingerprint and thumbprint leaves.

5 Add red thumbprint leaves next and then yellow prints for the outer leaves.

WHEN YOUR TREE IS FINISHED, TRY ADDING SOME THUMBPRINT BIRDS...

Tweet!
Tweet!

Tweet!
Tweet!

15

HALLOWEEN Handprints

DRACULA

1 Mix two colors. Quickly paint your fingers black and the palm of your hand pink (as shown).

2 Make a handprint on white paper.

3 Cut out black paper shapes for Dracula's cape and his collar. Glue in place.

4 Cut out shapes for his bow tie, eyes, and nose. Glue in place. Cut out Dracula's fangs.

5 Use marker to draw his eyes, mouth, and nostrils. Glue his fangs in place.

SOME MORE HALLOWEEN HANDPRINT IDEAS FOR YOU TO TRY!

SCARY BAT

CREEPY SPIDER

BLACK CAT

SPOOKY GHOST

17

MONSTER
thumbprints

SPARKY

1 Make a thumbprint for Sparky's head and another for his body.

2 Use a fine marker to draw in his eye, mouth, teeth, nostrils, ears, legs, and feet.

3 Draw in Sparky's arms and hands. Add his spiky tail. Paint his eye and teeth white.

CHISEL

1 Make two thumbprints, one for Chisel's head and the other for his body (as shown).

2 Use a fine marker to draw in his eye, mouth, teeth, legs, and feet.

3 Draw in his horns, arms, and hands. Paint in his teeth and mouth.

18

PINCER

1 Make a thumbprint for Pincer's head, another for her neck, and two for her body.

2 Use a fine marker to draw in her eyes, long snout, fangs, and horns.

3 Draw in Pincer's arms, hands, and antennae. Add lots of legs and feet. Paint her eyes and fangs white.

Roar!

SOME MORE THUMBPRINT MONSTER IDEAS FOR YOU TO TRY!

SPANNER

WIDGET

SPROCKET

SNIPS

19

DINOSAUR
Fingerprints and Thumbprints

DIPLODOCUS

1 Make a fingerprint for Diplodocus' head and a thumbprint for Diplodocus' body.

2 Use a fine marker to draw in his long, thin neck and his sturdy legs.

3 Add his tail, eyes, nostrils, mouth, and a tasty leaf for him to eat.

TRICERATOPS

1 Make two thumbprints: one for Triceratops' head and the other for his body.

2 Use a fine marker to draw in his head and neck frill. Add eyes and his mouth.

3 Draw in Triceratops' horns, legs, and tail. Paint his horn white.

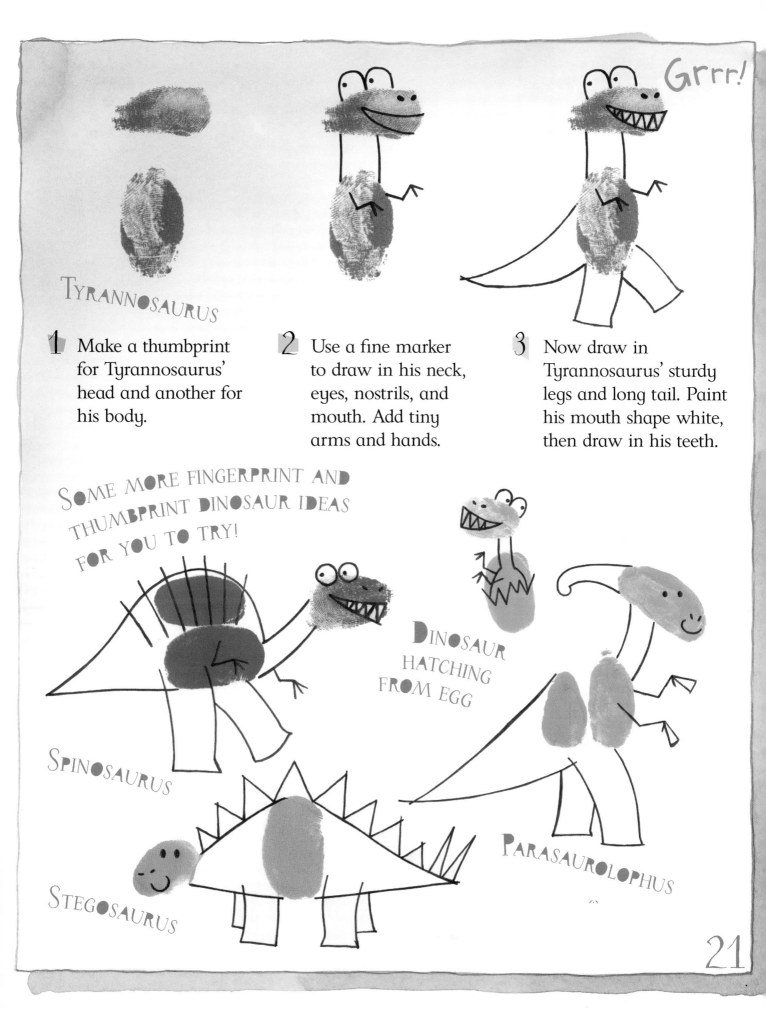

Grrr!

TYRANNOSAURUS

1 Make a thumbprint for Tyrannosaurus' head and another for his body.

2 Use a fine marker to draw in his neck, eyes, nostrils, and mouth. Add tiny arms and hands.

3 Now draw in Tyrannosaurus' sturdy legs and long tail. Paint his mouth shape white, then draw in his teeth.

SOME MORE FINGERPRINT AND THUMBPRINT DINOSAUR IDEAS FOR YOU TO TRY!

SPINOSAURUS

DINOSAUR HATCHING FROM EGG

STEGOSAURUS

PARASAUROLOPHUS

COLLAGE Thumbprint

1 Make some thumbprints. Pick out the clearest one.

2 Study its pattern to make a much bigger drawing of it on paper.

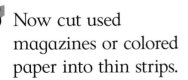

3 Now cut used magazines or colored paper into thin strips.

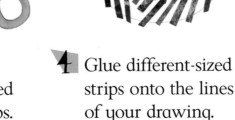

4 Glue different-sized strips onto the lines of your drawing.

5 Now cut around your unique thumbprint shape.

Finished!

23

ROCKET Handprint

Zoom!

1 Keeping your thumb and fingers quite close together, make a handprint.

2 Use a marker to draw in the shape of a rocket's nose cone.

3 Draw in shapes for the rocket's fins. Add a circle at the base of each fin.

4 Draw in a window and add a pointed tip to the nose cone. Add some exhaust flames.

5 Now use markers to color in the rocket. Add some black dots for rivets.

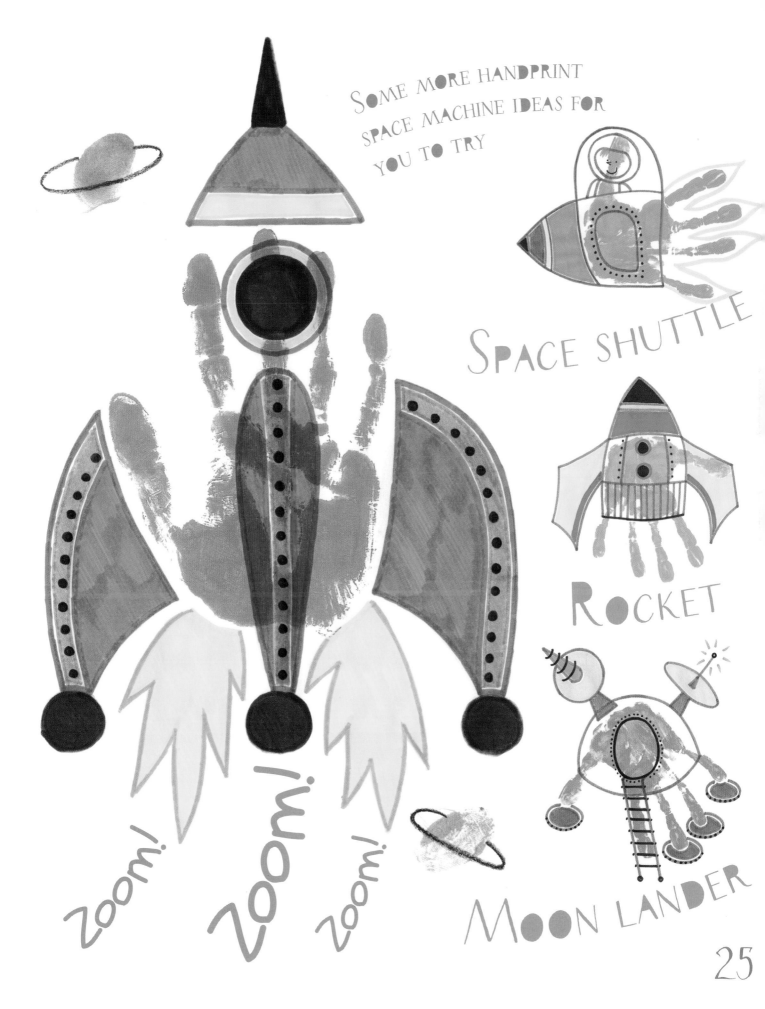

SOME MORE HANDPRINT
SPACE MACHINE IDEAS FOR
YOU TO TRY

SPACE SHUTTLE

ROCKET

ZOOM! ZOOM! ZOOM!

MOON LANDER

25

FESTIVE TREE
Handprints

1 Use green paper and dark green paint to make ten handprints.

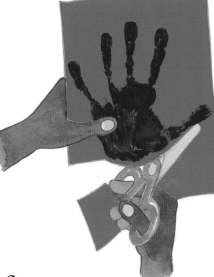

2 Cut around each handprint shape.

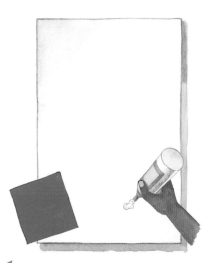

3 Cut a square of red paper. Glue it onto a large sheet of white paper (as shown).

4 Arrange the first four handprints above it and glue in place.

5 Glue three handprints on to make the next overlapping layer.

26

6 Glue two handprints on next, and then the last on the top.

CUT OUT A PAPER STAR AND SOME SMALL PAPER CIRCLES FOR DECORATIONS. GLUE IN PLACE.

3D HAND
Optical Illusion

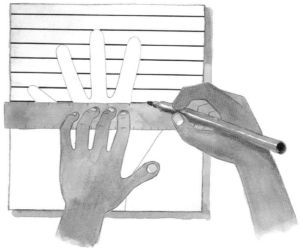

1 Rest your hand on a sheet of white paper and draw around it.

2 Using a ruler and black marker, draw horizontal lines across the page. Do not draw over your hand shape.

3 Now fill in the gaps using curved lines that appear to go up and over the shape of your hand.

4 Now use a different colored marker to draw a continuous line below each black line.

5 Add yet another set of colored lines under the last ones.

6 Finish off by coloring the remainder bright yellow. Erase any pencil lines.

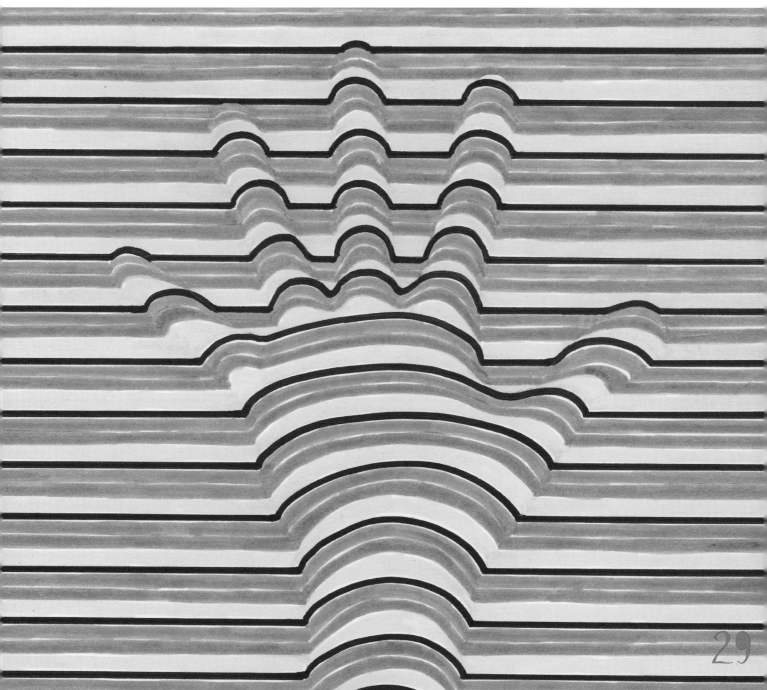

29

MORE FUN IDEAS
for Hand and Footprints

GIRAFFE

MONKEY

CRAB

FLAMINGO

PIRATE

REINDEER

GLOSSARY

3D a solid shape that has three dimensions—length, width, and height.

Collage artwork that is made by combining different materials such as cloth and paper on a flat surface.

Fangs teeth that are long, sharp, and pointed.

Festive when a festival occasion is joyful and fun.

Nose cone a protective cone on the front of a rocket or aeroplane.

Optical illusion use of color, light, and patterns to create images that trick the brain into seeing something in a different way.

Wreath flowers, leaves, or stems arranged into a ring-shape and used for decoration.

INDEX